Around the World

The Story of Tenzing Norgay

Paul May

Contents

OXFORD
UNIVERSITY PRESS

OXFORD
UNIVERSITY PRESS

Great Clarendon Street, Oxford OX2 6DP

Oxford University Press is a department of the University of Oxford.
It furthers the University's objective of excellence in research, scholarship,
and education by publishing worldwide in

Oxford   New York

Auckland Cape Town Dar es Salaam Hong Kong Karachi
Kuala Lumpur Madrid Melbourne Mexico City Nairobi
New Delhi Shanghai Taipei Toronto

With offices in
Argentina Austria Brazil Chile Czech Republic France Greece
Guatemala Hungary Italy Japan Poland Portugal Singapore
South Korea Switzerland Thailand Turkey Ukraine Vietnam

Oxford is a registered trade mark of Oxford University Press
in the UK and in certain other countries

British Library Cataloguing in Publication Data

Data available

ISBN: 978-0-19-919531-2

20 19 18 17 16 15

True Stories Pack 1 (one of each title) ISBN 978-0-19-919537-4
True Stories Pack 1 Class Pack (six of each title) ISBN 978-0-19-919536-7

Acknowledgements

The publisher would like to thank the following for permission to
reproduce photographs:

Corbis/Bettman: pp 1, 23 (bottom); Corbis/Hulton Deutsch Collection: p 3;
Corbis/Craig Lovell: p 15; Royal Geographical Society: pp 17, 23 (top)

Front Cover background photo: Corbis/Galen Rowell;
Inset photo: Corbis/Hulton Deutsch Collection
Back cover. Royal Geographical Society

Illustrations are by Martin Salisbury
Map is by Stefan Chabluk

Printed in China by Imago

Introduction

In May 1953 two men reached the top of Mount Everest, the highest mountain in the world.

One of the men was called Tenzing Norgay. He came from a tiny village in Nepal at the very foot of the mountain. This is Tenzing's story.

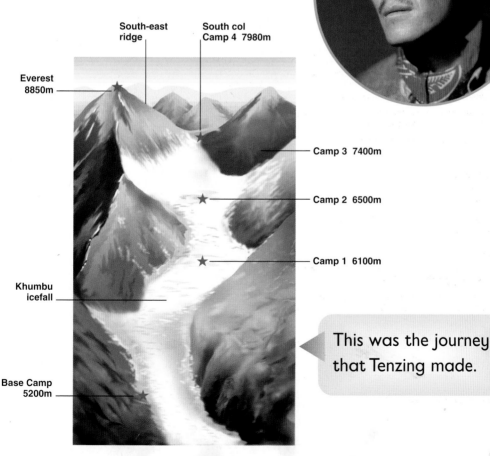

Everest 8850m

South-east ridge

South col
Camp 4 7980m

Camp 3 7400m

Camp 2 6500m

Camp 1 6100m

Khumbu icefall

Base Camp 5200m

This was the journey that Tenzing made.

Chapter 1

Tenzing's Dream

Tenzing Norgay was a **Sherpa** boy. From his
village he could see a tall mountain.
He dreamed of climbing to the very top.
  "I could see the whole world
from there," he thought.

Tenzing asked his mother about the mountain.

"The mountain is called **Chomolungma**," she told him. "It is so high that even the birds cannot fly over it."

"But maybe I could climb it one day," said Tenzing.

"Maybe," laughed his mother.

One day men came from a faraway
country called Britain.

"We want to climb Mount Everest," they
said, "the mountain you call Chomolungma.
We want Sherpas to help us."

"I'll go with you," said Tenzing.

But his mother laughed.

"You are far too small," she said.

Running Away

Again and again, men tried to reach the top of Chomolungma. Many climbers died in the ice and snow.

When Tenzing was older he said, "I know I can climb the mountain."

"You are mad," said his mother. "I won't let you go."

So Tenzing ran away from home!

When Tenzing arrived at the climbers' camp, he cut his hair and borrowed some clothes.

"You look strong," the climbers said. "We will give you a job."

The men gave Tenzing strange clothes
to wear. He ate strange food out of tin
cans, but he was happy.

He was going to Chomolungma at last!

Chapter 3

Chomolungma

The climbers walked for 100 miles.

They climbed up and up through the snow, but then they stopped.

Chomolungma was still above them, touching the sky.

"I want to go higher," said Tenzing.

"Not this year," said the climbers. "But we will come back."

Many years later, climbers came from Switzerland. They found a new way to get to Chomolungma.

Tenzing climbed with one of them. The two men climbed very high. The air was thin and it was hard to breathe. They had no food or water left.

Outside, the wind roared like a thousand tigers. The men stayed awake all night and shivered.

The next day they tried to climb higher. They could almost see the top, but they were cold and very tired.

"We must turn back," they said, "or we will die."

Chapter 4

To the Mountain Again

Tenzing was exhausted. He had to go to hospital.

But then a letter came from Britain.

"Please climb with us again," it said.

"You are too weak to go," said Tenzing's wife. "You will die."

"I would rather die on Chomolungma than lie here in this bed," Tenzing replied.

10th March 1953

Tenzing went to meet the climbers and other Sherpas. They set off carrying heavy loads across hills, valleys and rushing rivers.

The monastery in the mountains

26th March

At last, the climbers came to a **monastery**, high in the mountains.

The **lamas** gave them tea made with butter and salt.

"The goddess **Miyosanglangma** lives on Chomolungma," the lamas said. "We will ask her to let you climb the mountain."

Chapter 5

Crumbling Towers of Ice

23rd April

The climbers walked on and set up camp.

They looked for a way between the crumbling towers of ice. Deep cracks opened under their feet. All the climbers were scared.

Tenzing was climbing with a man called Edmund Hillary. Suddenly Hillary cried out, "TENZING!"

Hillary was sliding into a crack, but Tenzing was ready. Tenzing tied a rope around his ice-axe, and he held on to the rope.

He had saved Hillary's life.

After that day, Tenzing and Hillary always climbed together.

Crossing a dangerous crack in the ice.

Chapter 6

"Shall We Go On?"

27th May

Tenzing and Hillary climbed so high that they could see for 100 miles. They put up their tent on a narrow ledge.

Early the next morning they started to climb a snow cliff. Hillary slipped, and then Tenzing slipped too. They were both scared. If they fell, they would die.

"Shall we go on?" asked Hillary.
Tenzing looked up.
All his life he had dreamed of
climbing Chomolungma.
"I will go on if you will," he said.
So Hillary began to climb again.

Chapter 7

Into the Sky

At last they reached the top of the cliff.
More rock and snow towered above them.

The way was narrow, and steep slopes fell
away on both sides. They walked slowly, up
and up, into the sky.

Tenzing and Hillary stopped. Now there was a wall of icy rock above them.

"I can see a way," Hillary said.

They climbed over the rock and fell on the ground. They could hardly breathe.

"Look," said Hillary.

Up ahead was a gentle slope of snow. They began to walk and suddenly …

… all around them there was nothing but air. They had done it!

Tenzing hugged Hillary. He looked down and saw his village, miles below.

"Thank you, Miyosanglangma," he said to the goddess of the mountain. Then he buried sweets in the snow for her.

Tenzing's dream had come true at last. He had climbed Chomolungma – the highest mountain in the world.

Hillary took a photo of Tenzing.

Tenzing and Hillary were given medals.

Glossary

Chomolungma the name which Sherpas give to Mount Everest

lama a name for a holy man or monk

Miyosanglangma a goddess who the lamas believe lives on Chomolungma

monastery a building where monks or lamas live

Sherpa a group of people who live in a country called Nepal. Many Sherpas live near Mount Everest.

Index

24